Confidence Is...

by Diane M. Stortz

illustrated by Richard Bishop

STANDARD PUBLISHING
Cincinnati, Ohio   3667

Library of Congress Cataloging-in-Publication Data

Stortz, Diane M.
Confidence is—.

(I'm growing up series)
Summary: Defines self-confidence, discusses how it develops, and emphasizes that confidence can come from the individual's knowledge that he is important to God.
 1. Self-confidence—Juvenile literature. [1. Self-confidence. 2. Christian life] I. Bishop, Rich, ill. II. Title. III. Series.
BF575.S39S76 1987   158'.1   87-1885
ISBN 0-87403-322-5

Copyright © 1987 by The STANDARD PUBLISHING Company
Cincinnati, Ohio
Division of STANDEX INTERNATIONAL Corporation.
Printed in the U.S.A.

Confidence Is...

Can you remember the first time you rode a two-wheeler all by yourself? Can you remember learning to swim, or the first night you slept away from home?

How about the time you hit a home run, or when you got an A on the book report you read aloud, in front of the whole class?

How did you feel when you did those things—happy? proud? glad to be you? Those good feelings are what *confidence* is. Confidence is feeling good about being you.

These four people have something in common. Can you find what it is?

Moses wasn't much of a public speaker. But when God told him to talk to Pharaoh, he obeyed. And God used Moses to lead His people out of Egypt.

Joni Eareckson Tada was paralyzed from the neck down when she broke her neck in a diving accident. Today Joni draws with a pen held in her mouth, and she has written books and made record albums and a movie. She has a radio program and a ministry to other handicapped people.

When *Darrell Porter* was a catcher for the Milwaukee Brewers, he began taking drugs. He couldn't play his best, and he was traded to the Kansas City Royals. Darrell got help to stop taking drugs. In 1982, playing for the St. Louis Cardinals, he was named the Most Valuable Player in the World Series.

Abraham Lincoln was born in a log cabin. His family was poor, and Lincoln didn't have much education. But he read whatever books he could find, and when he grew up he trained himself to be a lawyer. Later, Lincoln was elected President of the United States.

What do Moses, Joni Eareckson Tada, Darrell Porter, and Abraham Lincoln have in common? They have *confidence!*

Having confidence is not the same thing as being conceited. In fact, people who talk about themselves all the time usually don't have any confidence at all. They try to make themselves look good by bragging or showing off.

Everyone needs confidence. Things don't always go the way we want them to. Maybe you didn't make the team, or get the part you wanted in the school play. Maybe you have asthma or diabetes or have to wear braces. Maybe you lose *every time* you play checkers with your big brothers. At times like these, it's important to remember all the things you *can* do, and have confidence in you.

Can you ...
   draw a picture?
   write a poem?
   climb a tree?
   throw a football?
   sing a song?
   bake a cake?
   build a birdhouse?
   play the piano?
   pack your lunch?
   grow a garden?
   groom your dog?

What else can you do?

Our *abilities,* the things we can do, help give us confidence. Confidence also comes from the people around us. Parents usually try to help their children feel good about themselves.

And when you make a mistake, they love you anyway.

Maybe you have a teacher who's given you confidence. When you didn't think you could learn long division, he said, "You can do it! I'll help you." And now long division is *easy*.

Or maybe you know a baseball coach, or a scout leader, or a Sunday-school teacher who has helped you have confidence.

Friends can help us have confidence too.

But there's an even more important reason why you can have confidence, and that is because you are so important to *God*. God loves you. He made you, and He knows all about you. God is with you everywhere you go, and He has a plan for your life.

God cares about what happens to you. He loves you so much that He sent Jesus to die on the cross to take away your sins. Jesus promised that He will always be your friend. With a friend like Jesus, you have the best kind of confidence there is.

When you have confidence, you can have fun doing things even if you're not the best. Having confidence helps you be happy for your friends when *they* win.

And when you have confidence, you can enjoy trying new things. You won't get upset if you can't do something just right the very first time.

When you have confidence, you can do things that are hard, like learning to play the violin,

Or scary, like learning to swim. When you have confidence, you don't give up. You keep on trying.

And one day you might play a solo with the symphony, or swim in the Olympics!

When you have confidence, you can help someone in trouble. You won't wait to see if anyone else is going to help. You'll do whatever needs to be done, right away.

When you have confidence, you can do what is right. If your friends are making fun of a teacher you like, you'll say, "She's not so bad. I like her." If *anyone* wants you to do *anything* you know is wrong, you can say no and mean it.

But no one feels good about himself *all* the time.

Even grown-ups sometimes think that nothing they do ever works out right.

It's OK to feel that way sometimes, but it isn't good to feel like that a lot. Tell someone else how you feel. You can talk to your parents, a teacher, or your minister, or to some other grown-up friend you know will listen.

So have confidence! You're a person made by God, who gave you special abilities. As you grow, He will help you find and follow His plan for your life.

And someday you may say to a child of your own, "Have confidence! *You can do it!*"